MW00966210

just

A LITTLE BOOK OF LIQUID FUN

Cheryl Charming

Photographs by Susan Bourgoin

Lyons Press
Guilford, Connecticut

An imprint of Globe Pequot Press

SHOTS

Copyright © 2010 by Morris Book Publishing, LLC

The following manufacturers/names appearing in *Just Shots* are trademarks:
Absolut®, Absolut® Citron, Absolut® Peppar, Amarula, Bacardi®, Baileys® Original Irish Cream, Bénédictine, Captain Morgan® Spiced Rum, Chambord®, Chambord® Liqueur Royale de France, Chartreuse, Cointreau®, Crown Royal® Canadian, Curaçao, Diageo, DiSaronno® Amaretto, Don Eduardo, Drambuie®, Frangelico®, Galliano, George Dickel, Goldschläger®, Gosling's Black Seal Rum, Grand Marnier®, Grey Goose®, Guinness® Stout, Irish Mist, Jack Daniel's, Jim Beam®, Johnnie Walker®, Jose Cuervo®, Kahlúa®, Ketel One®, Licor 43, Malibu Coconut Rum, Midori®, Myers's Original Dark Rum, Navan®, Red Bull®, Rose's®, Sakura, Seagram's®, Smirnoff®, Southern Comfort®, St-Germain Elderflower, Stolichnaya®, Tabasco®, Wild Turkey

The photos on the following pages are courtesy of Shutterstock.com: iv © Fedor Kondratenko; 20 © Mihai Simonia; 37 © Michael Ransburg; 50 © Elzbieta Sekowska; 53 © eyespeak; 68 © Michael C. Gray; 86 © Palachinka; 90 © wojciechpusz; 94 © Glue Stock; 102 and 110 © Monika Olszewska.

Prop Credits:
Bar tools and products provided by www.barproducts.com.
Cocktail sticks, picks, straws, and drink decoration novelties provided by Spirit Foodservice, Inc. (www.spirit foodservice.com).

Text design by Georgiana Goodwin

Library of Congress Cataloging-in-Publication Data is available on file.

ISBN 978-1-59921-896-0

Printed in China

10 9 8 7 6 5 4 3 2 1

Contents

Producing the perfect shot or shooter, no matter the type or flavor, will require some finesse and equipment on the part of its maker.

Here's a rundown of what you'll need and how you'll use it to mix impressive, tasty shots.

POURERS

One of the best tools you can invest in is a bottle pourer. Twisting off spirit bottle lids and "glug-glugging" spirits work well for a neat drink (neat means a drink poured straight from the bottle into a glass without ice), but for precise and smooth control, a pourer is the best choice. Simply screw off a bottle lid and then push the pourer into the bottle. If your bottle has a wide mouth, then you'll have to buy a wide pourer. If you're using pourers for a party, just keep your bottle lids until you are finished, then screw the lids back on. After you are comfortable with pouring, bump it up a notch and try a long pour. Simply raise the bottle higher, creating a longer stream of spirit. Then you can graduate to reverse pouring, which is grabbing the neck of the bottle in reverse and pouring.

Pourers add a professional touch when making cocktails. Use them in bottles that are used most often. Pourers come with options such as color, size, and material (plastic or metal). When pouring, flip up the bottle quickly and vertically. Practice with a bottle of water. Cut (downward movement when finished pouring) quickly downward in a smooth motion.

Using exact measures in a cocktail is crucial, and that's why jiggers and measuring devices are helpful. There are many sizes to choose from, especially from the two-ended jiggers.

The most professional bartenders use jiggers and measuring glasses for accuracy. Invest in a couple of jiggers of different sizes. For control, rest the edge of the jigger on or near the lip of the glass so that it creates one fluid movement of pouring and dumping. Try to rinse out jiggers as you go, especially when using creamy liqueurs.

LAYERING

Practice layering at home with ingredients from your kitchen such as oils, vinegars, water, and juice. Layering requires a steady hand. You can break the fall of the liquid with practically anything. Most bars use

a spoon or cherry. When layering several spirits and liqueurs or several drinks, have all your bottles set in a row and ready to go ●

Stylized Layering

Layering takes a bit of practice, but after you get it you got it. An advanced and stylized way to layer is to use a disc-ended bar spoon. The disc end goes into the glass, and you pour the spirit or liqueur on the spiral handle. It travels and spirals down into the glass.

Shot glasses come in a plethora of styles and can be made of almost anything.

Some people even have a collection of shot glasses because wherever you travel you find them in souvenir shops. Novelty shot and shooter glasses are endless. You can buy necklace shot glasses, shot glass rings, test tube shots, glasses that light up, and glasses that are split in two so you can pour one spirit on one side of the divider and something else on the other. They can also be found in practically any shape imaginable, such as boots, bullets, body parts, animals, and cacti. Edible shot glasses can be made, and glasses made of chocolate, candy, gummy bears, or ice or any liquid that will freeze can be bought. You can even find checkerboards and chessboards that use shot and shooter glasses. The standard shot glass will measure 1–2 ounces, while the standard shooter glass will measure 2–5 ounces.

Sometimes pony and cordial glasses are used for shot and shooter glasses. You'll find that they're often used at nice dinner parties. A pony glass is a cordial glass, but not all cordial glasses can be called "pony

Brad Rodgers holds the Guinness world record for the largest shot glass collection. He lives in Las Vegas and has around twelve thousand shot glasses, but three thousand of them are duplicates, so those don't count. Guinness has him on record as owning almost nine thousand shot glasses. The most valuable shot glasses are the official glasses of the Kentucky Derby.

glasses" because of their measurement. All liqueurs and cordials such as crèmes, creams, and schnapps can be poured into cordial glasses. In bar terms, the

word pony is a unit of measurement of 1 ounce, so pony glasses will always measure 1 ounce. Pony glasses are always stemmed. Cordial glasses can range in size from 1 ounce to 3 ounces. A serving of cordial or liqueur would be served in a cordial glass.

Shooters are often strained into rocks glasses, which are meant to hold a portion of spirit without mixer over ice. Rocks glasses come in a variety of shapes and sizes and measure 5–7 ounces ●

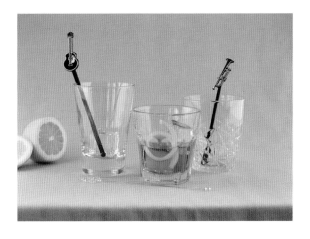

THE ORIGINAL

DISTILLING KETEL Nº1

Ketel One®
VODKA

Handcrafted in small
batches, using
traditional recipes at
the Nolet Distillery
in Holland

Founded 1691.

40% Alc.
by Vol.

Contents
750ml

IMPORTED

Personal taste has a lot to do with how you mix your cocktails.

There's a wide range in the quality and flavorings of spirits and liqueurs, and a little bit of experimenting will help you find your preferences and introduce you to many new and tasty options.

VODKA

Many believe vodka has been around since the 1300s, but it was not like the clean, clear vodka of today. It's believed that makers infused it with herbs, flowers, and fruits.

Smirnoff vodka was the first to use charcoal filtering in 1870. Today Smirnoff is owned by drinks giant Diageo and is the top-selling vodka in the world.

ULTRA-PREMIUM VODKA

High-end, boutique, and ultra-premium vodkas hit the market around the millennium.

Master marketer Sidney Frank is responsible for introducing Grey Goose vodka, the first heavily marketed ultra-premium vodka. High-end vodkas focus on sleek and modern bottle design and multiple filtering. Ketel One vodka has won many blind vodka taste tests.

FLAVORED VODKA

Absolut introduced the first infused/flavored vodka in 1986 called "Absolut Peppar." It's flavored with three types of peppers, making it perfect for a Bloody Mary. Almost every vodka brand has a line of flavored vodka. Absolut Citron exploded the vodka infusion world with lemon drops and cosmopolitans. Second to flavor its vodkas was Stolichnaya.

RUM

Rum can be made from sugarcane or from its by-products: sugarcane juice and molasses. Since the 1600s, rum has been used for trading, drinking, bribing, and even paying wages.

LIGHT RUM

Light rum is also known as "silver," "white," or "platinum rum." Light rum doesn't require aging and is usually bottled after distillation. Brazil makes a rum from Brazilian sugarcane that they call "cachaça" (pronounced ka-SHAH-sa). The popular cocktail called the "caipirinha" (pronounced kai-pee-REEN-ya) is made with it. Bacardi is the most popular light rum worldwide.

GOLD RUM

Gold rum is sometimes called "amber rum." The gold color comes from the rum's being aged in wooden barrels. Some gold rums make great mixing rums, and others are excellent for sipping like a fine cognac. It mostly depends on aging. Some premium gold rums are actually blends rum that have been aged up to ten years.

DARK RUM

Dark rum is also known as "black rum." Myers's Original Dark Rum is the most popular dark rum in the world. It's made from 100 percent Jamaican molasses. Two dark rums are used in famous recipes: Gosling's Black Seal Rum in a dark 'n stormy and Myers's Dark Rum in a planter's punch. Dark rum is often used as a floater on top of a tropical drink.

FLAVORED RUM

Flavors include coconut, banana, mango, raspberry, vanilla, spiced, pineapple, citron, passion fruit, orange, and lime.

In 1984, Captain Morgan Spiced Rum became the first flavored rum available in America.

Malibu Coconut Rum was released in the early 1980s as well but classified as a liqueur with rum and coconut flavorings. Today the distillery claims that it's now made with rum.

TEQUILA

The numero uno thing to know about tequila is that by law it can be produced only in the Tequila region of Mexico. The numero dos thing to know is that in order for a label to say "tequila" it must be made from at least 51 percent blue agave. If it's not, then it's called a "mixto" (this is a good example of Mezcal).

BLANCO TEQUILA

Blanco is also called "silver" or "white tequila." Most times blanco tequila is either bottled straight out of the still or filtered, then bottled. If stored, blanco tequila must not be kept longer than sixty days in stainless steel tanks for no aging. One hundred percent agave blanco tequila is an excellent choice to use for margaritas.

REPOSADO TEQUILA

Reposado is a blanco that has been aged in white oak casks for two to twelve months. It has a mellow yellow color and taste. The gold color of a reposado comes from aging in the wood casks. Reposado means "rested" (as in "rested in barrels"). Reposado is the highest-quality tequila that will still taste good in a margarita. It has a balance between bite and smoothness.

AÑEJO TEQUILA

Añejo is a blanco tequila that has been aged for more than one year. High-quality añejos are aged up to three years. Añejo that is aged up to eight years is called "reserva." There is controversy over letting

tequila age this long because the oak begins to overwhelm the agave flavor. Añejo means "old."

Today whiskey/whisky is made all over the world in places such as India, Japan, Germany, France, and Russia, but the four most prominent countries that have been making whiskey/whisky for centuries are Scotland, Ireland, America, and Canada.

IRISH WHISKEY

Ireland makes blended, single-malt, grain, and pure pot still whiskey. There are only three distilleries in the entire country of Ireland. Irish whiskey is made from malt that is dried in sealed ovens and usually distilled three times. There are two popular Irish whiskey-based liqueurs: Baileys Original Irish Cream and Irish Mist.

SCOTCH WHISKY

Scotland makes blended Scotch whisky and single-malt whisky. Scotch whisky is known for its smoky flavor, which comes from drying malted barley over open peat fires. Scotland is divided into four geo-graphical flavors: Lowlands, Highlands, Speyside, and the Islands. A popular Scotch-based liqueur from Scotland is Drambuie. It's made from heather honey and herbs.

CANADIAN WHISKY

Canada blends its whisky for a smoother taste. Often Canada calls its whisky "rye" but doesn't follow strict laws about how much rye must be in the whisky. Crown Royal Canadian whisky was made by Sea-gram's especially for Queen Elizabeth's visit in 1939.

Remember, Canada and Scotland spell whisky without an e. America and Ireland spell whiskey with an e.

AMERICAN WHISKEY

America produces five kinds of whiskey: bourbon, corn, rye, blended, and Tennessee.

By federal law bourbon can be made only in America and made with at least 51 percent American corn. Only bourbon made in Kentucky can have the words "Kentucky bourbon" on a label. In 1964, an act

of Congress declared bourbon as "America's Native Spirit" as well as the country's official distilled spirit.

LIQUEURS

By the civilized nineteenth century, liqueurs were drunk as an apéritif (before-dinner drink) or as an after-dinner digestive drink. Italians have been known for a long time to drink Sambuca before dinner and shots of Limoncello after. Other popular Italian liqueurs include Tuaca, Galliano, Frangelico, and DiSaronno Amaretto. Germans are known to drink peppermint schnapps after dinner, but the most popular liqueur from Germany is Jägermeister.

Almost every country in the world has at least one liqueur. Popular French liqueurs include Chambord, Cointreau, Chartreuse, St-Germain Elderflower, Grand Marnier, Bénédictine, and the crème family. Spain has Licor 43, Greece has Ouzo, the U.S. has Southern Comfort, Switzerland has Goldschläger, Jamaica has Tia Maria, Mexico has Kahlúa, Japan has Sakura, South Africa has Amarula, and the list goes on and on.

There are over five hundred commercial liqueurs in the world. Liqueurs are sweet flavor-infused spirits and can also be called "cordials." Liqueurs can be low-proof, high-proof, cream, crème, or schnapps.

CREAM LIQUEURS

Cream liqueurs are made with dairy cream and a spirit base. Baileys Original Irish Cream is the most popular cream liqueur in the world. It was the first cream and paved the way for many others.

CRÈME LIQUEURS

Crème is a French word that is pronounced "krem." Crèmes have a lot of sugar added to them, which results in a syrupy consistency. The most popular crèmes are crème de cacao (light and dark) and crème de menthe (white/clear and green). Other crèmes include crème de banana, crème de cassis (black currants), and crème de Yvette (violets).

SCHNAPPS

The word *schnapps* is of German descent and means "swallow." Schnapps is usually a high-proof liqueur because it is made from fermented fruits, grain, or herbs, then distilled. True German schnapps does not have added sugar. American schnapps tends to be very sweet. This is because sugar is added after distillation ●

Before cocktails, there were shots. It was simple, really: a shot of hard liquor alongside a brew.

Those cowboys sitting at dusty tables in local saloons probably never knew how hip it was to order a bottle for the table. Today they call it "bottle service," and it can be found in trendy nightclubs the world over. And although shots have changed in flavor, color, and names, the purpose remains the same: to have fun with your friends.

A word to the wise: at a nightclub, it's best to order shots, not shooters. Around the millennium, nightclub bartenders began shaking up shooters and pouring them into shot-sized glasses. The alcohol portion for a shot or shooter should be 1–1 1/2 ounces. These bartenders are pouring 1 1/2 ounces of alcohol into the shaker, adding mixer, shaking, then straining out five to eight shots from that one portion. And they'll charge $5–$9 for each! All this can be avoided by learning to make some dazzling shots at home ●

Shot of Tequila

INGREDIENTS

Lime (or lemon) slice
salt to rim glass
1$^1/_2$ ounces tequila of choice

1. Wet part of a shot glass with a lime slice, then dip it in salt.

2. Pour tequila into the glass.

3. Lick the salt, drink the tequila, then bite into the meat of the lime.

> In some countries, people substitute the salt for cinnamon and the lime for orange when shooting aged tequila. And around the millennium, the trendy way to shoot tequila is chilled, which is another way to avoid tasting the tequila.

Prairie Fire

INGREDIENTS

1½ ounces tequila of choice
5 dashes Tabasco

1. Pour the tequila into a shot glass.

2. Dash in five hard jerks of Tabasco.

> A dash of Tabasco helps mask the taste of tequila.

Bull Fight

INGREDIENTS

5 ounces coffee liqueur
$\frac{1}{2}$ ounce Sambuca
$\frac{1}{2}$ ounce gold tequila
2 dashes Tabasco

1. Slowly layer the first three ingredients in order into a shot glass.

2. Dash the Tabasco.

Flat Tire

INGREDIENTS

3/4 ounce black Sambuca
3/4 ounce tequila of choice
Ice

1. Shake the black Sambuca and tequila with ice.

2. Strain into a shot glass.

Tequila passion shots have been popular since the 1980s. To prep, you lick a body part of another person (hopefully a person you've known for a bit), then sprinkle salt on the moistness. Next, place a lime wedge meat side out in the person's mouth. Now you're ready to lick the salt, drink the shot, and suck the lime.

Lemon Drop Shot

INGREDIENTS

Sugar to rim glass
1½ ounces citrus vodka
Ice

1. Rim a shot glass with sugar.

2. Shake vodka with ice.

3. Strain into the glass.

Here's a top-shelf Lemon Drop Shot spinoff for your special guests. You'll need 1½ ounces of chilled citrus vodka, ½ ounce of Grand Marnier, a lemon slice, a teaspoon of sugar, a match, a saucer, and a shot glass. Lay the lemon slice on the saucer and cover with the sugar. Pour some Grand Marnier on top of the sugar to make it flammable, then light. As the sugar is being crystallized into the lemon, chill a shot of citrus vodka and pour it into the shot glass. By the time you're done, the flame will have died down. Now drink the chilled shot, then bite into the warm, sugary lemon. Pick up the saucer and pour the leftover Grand Marnier into the shot glass and drink it, too. So decadent!

Russian Roulette

INGREDIENTS

1½ ounces vodka
Ice
Orange slice
Sugar
¼ ounce 151 rum or Grand Marnier

1. Shake the vodka with ice and strain into a shot glass.

2. Place an orange slice on top of the glass with sugar and rum on top of the orange.

3. Light the orange, then wait until the flame dies out.

4. Pick up the orange, drink, and then bite the sugary, warm orange.

Always take strong precautions when using fire. Long sleeves, long hair, and paper napkins nearby are just a few of the things people forget about. Always think ahead as if you're childproofing the area and never consume anything with flames.

Chocolate Cake

INGREDIENTS

Ice
1 ounce lemon vodka
$1/2$ ounces Frangelico hazelnut liqueur
Sugared lemon wedge garnish

1. Shake the ingredients with ice.

2. Strain into a shot glass.

3. Drink, then bite into a lemon dipped in sugar.

Weird Cake

There's not any chocolate in the Chocolate Cake shot, but it tastes like it. This shot showed up around the millennium. It's one of those weird "Twilight Zone" mouth sensations. It uses citrus vodka and hazelnut liqueur and ends with a sugared lemon. The weird part is that when you bite into the lemon, it tastes like chocolate cake. Weird.

Arizona Anti-Freeze

INGREDIENTS

$\frac{1}{3}$ ounce vodka
$\frac{1}{3}$ ounce Midori
$\frac{1}{3}$ ounce sweet and sour mix

1. Shake the vodka, Midori, and mix with ice.

2. Strain into a shot glass.

More on Vodka

Vodka provides a blank canvas that allows much experimentation. Companies infuse it with flavors, make it from organic materials, color it black, or harvest chunks of icebergs to use as their water. College students have even been known to run cheap vodka through a water filter a few times to make it taste like premium vodka.

B-52

INGREDIENTS

$\frac{1}{2}$ ounce Kahlúa coffee liqueur
$\frac{1}{2}$ ounce Baileys Original Irish Cream
$\frac{1}{2}$ ounce Grand Marnier

1. Layer the liqueurs in the order given into a shot glass.

The B-52 shot was named after the U.S. B-52 Stratofortress bombers built for the Air Force in 1954. President George H. W. Bush took them off alert duty in 1991. Many people have claimed to have created the shot, but the only real fact agreed upon so far is that its birth was in the 1970s.

Whipped Cream Shot

INGREDIENTS

$3/4$ ounce coffee liqueur
$3/4$ ounce Irish cream
Whipped cream garnish

1. Slowly layer the two ingredients in order into a shot glass.

2. Top with whipped cream.

3. Drink without using your hands.

> You can adjust liqueur portions to the size of the shot glass you are using.

Buttery Irishman

INGREDIENTS

$3/4$ ounce butterscotch schnapps
$3/4$ ounce Irish cream

1. Pour the butterscotch schnapps into a shot glass.

2. Slowly layer the Irish cream on top of the schnapps.

Irish Cream Shots

Irish cream shots first started in 1974 and there are many other liqueurs that mix well with it. In the same way you layer the Irish cream on top of butterscotch schnapps to make a Buttery Irishman, you can replace the schnapps with Sambuca, crème de banana, or cinnamon schnapps.

Three Wise Men

INGREDIENTS

$\frac{1}{2}$ ounce Jack Daniel's Tennessee whiskey
$\frac{1}{2}$ ounce Johnnie Walker Scotch whisky
$\frac{1}{2}$ ounce Jim Beam Bourbon
Ice

1. Shake the three whiskeys with ice.

2. Strain into a shot glass.

3. Can be served neat as well.

The novelty of this shot strictly plays off the name of the particular alcohol used. This foundation recipe is pretty solid because a tower of shots can be built on top. For example, if you add Wild Turkey Bourbon, then the shot is called "Three Wise Men Go Hunting." Add Jose Cuervo into the mix, and it turns into Three Wise Men Go to Mexico. Here are more to try. Three Wise Men Go Sailing = add Captain Morgan spiced rum; Three Wise Men Go Nutty = add Amaretto; Three Wise Men Go Goose Hunting with a Friend = add Grey Goose vodka and George Dickel Bourbon; Three Wise Men Triple Date = add brandy, ginger liqueur, and Tia Maria; you get the idea.

Monkey on Jack's Back

INGREDIENTS

¾ ounce banana liqueur
¾ ounce Jack Daniel's Tennessee whiskey

1. Pour the banana liqueur into a shot glass.

2. Slowly layer the Jack Daniel's on top of the liqueur.

3. Can be served chilled and up as well.

Jack Daniel was the youngest of thirteen children. His mother died when he was two, and after a few years he felt neglected and ran away to the neighbors, where he learned how to make whiskey. By age thirteen he owned his own distillery. He stood 5 feet 2 inches and never married or had children. He died in 1911 at age sixty-five.

Snowshoe

INGREDIENTS

Ice
$^3/_4$ ounce Wild Turkey Bourbon
$^3/_4$ ounce peppermint schnapps

1. Shake the ingredients with ice.

2. Strain into a shot glass.

Stinging Nettle

INGREDIENTS

1 ounce Irish whiskey
$1/2$ ounce green (or white) crème de menthe

1. Shake ingredients with ice.

2. Strain into a shot glass and garnish with a mint leaf.

Mindbender

INGREDIENTS

$1/4$ ounce bourbon whiskey
$3/4$ ounce Chambord

1. Shake the ingredients with ice.

2. Strain into a shot glass.

3. Can be served neat as well.

American Flag

INGREDIENTS

1¼ ounce white crème de cacao
Few drops of grenadine
¼ ounce blue Curaçao

1. Pour the white crème de cacao into a shot glass.

2. Pour the grenadine in, and it will sink to the bottom.

3. Slowly layer the blue Curaçao on top.

The American Flag shot can also be called by its two nicknames, "Old Glory" and "Star-Spangled Banner." If you like the latter, then cut a star fruit and set it on the rim just for fun. This shot—when drunk in one gulp—tastes exactly like a chocolate-covered cherry. It's great for patriotic parties. If you stir it with a cocktail straw, then it turns purple, and you can say that you can see the purple mountain majesties.

Mexican Flag

INGREDIENTS

$\frac{1}{2}$ ounce grenadine
$\frac{1}{2}$ ounce green crème de menthe
$\frac{1}{2}$ ounce half-and-half

1. Pour the grenadine into a shot glass.

2. Slowly layer the green crème de menthe on top of the grenadine.

3. Slowly layer the half-and-half on top of the crème de menthe.

> The Mexican Flag shot is perfect for a fiesta or a Cinco de Mayo party. The colors of the Mexican flag (red, green, and white) have changed through the years, but today they mean hope, unity, and the blood of the national heroes.

Irish Flag

INGREDIENTS

$1/2$ ounce green crème de menthe
$1/2$ ounce Irish cream
$1/2$ ounce Irish whiskey

1. Pour the green crème de menthe into a shot glass.

2. Slowly layer the Irish cream on top.

3. Slowly layer the Irish whiskey on top of the Irish cream.

Alaskan Flag

INGREDIENTS

³/₄ ounce chilled Goldschläger cinnamon
schnapps
³/₄ ounce blue Curaçao

1. Pour the Goldschläger into a shot glass.

2. Slowly layer the blue Curaçao on top.

When making the Alaskan Flag shot, it's best to have the ingredients chilled beforehand but don't shake them with ice. Simply put the bottle of Goldschläger and blue Curaçao in the freezer until you are ready to make the shot. Also, having the alcohol freezing cold will really make you feel like you are in Alaska.

Pirate Treasure

INGREDIENTS

$^3/_4$ ounce chilled Goldschläger
$^3/_4$ ounce chilled Captain Morgan Spiced Rum

1. Pour the Goldschläger into a shot glass.

2. Slowly layer the Captain Morgan Spiced Rum on top.

Many shots just taste better ice cold, and the Pirate Treasure is an example, so make sure to chill the bottles in the freezer first. Also, the novelty of the shot is that the Captain Morgan Spiced Rum is amber in color to represent sand, and the pirate gold is buried under the sand.

S'mores

INGREDIENTS

$1/2$ ounce vanilla vodka or rum
$1/4$ ounce butterscotch schnapps
$1/4$ ounce Irish cream
Chocolate shot glass*
1 Teddy Grahams bear for garnish
Splash 151 rum
2 minimarshmallows on a toothpick

1. Pour the first three ingredients into a chocolate shot glass.

2. Set the Teddy Grahams bear on top, then top with 151 rum. Light.

3. Roast marshmallows, blow out the flame.

4. Drink, bite chocolate glass, then eat the marshmallows.

*See page 120 for making your own chocolate shot glasses.

Flu Shot

INGREDIENTS

3/4 ounce melon liqueur
3/4 ounce Jägermeister
Ice

1. Shake the ingredients with ice.

2. Pour into a shot glass.

Give Your Best Shot

Be the life of the party or impress your friends by investing in some reusable plastic shooter syringes. Of course, you can fill a syringe with your choice of shots, but the flu shot fits the bill perfectly. Make a batch by multiplying the recipe. Place them in a bowl or bucket of ice so they stay chilled.

Shots and shooters have two things in common: Both are drunk in one gulp, and both have the same alcohol content. The difference is that shots are 100 percent alcohol, and shooters have a mixer added to them. And shooters require a slightly larger glass because of the mixer and the water, which melts during shaking.

Kamikazes and Boilermakers are classified as Shooters because they contain mixers. Kamikaze is a Japanese word. *Kami* means "God/divine," and *kaze* means "wind." The Kamikaze shooter is believed to have been named after kamikaze pilots. The Boilermaker started with two simple parts: a shot of whiskey followed by a chaser of beer. Then one day someone somewhere—probably after a hard day's work as a boilermaker—was so tired he decided to just drop the shot in the beer and then drink it. Today a Boilermaker has turned into a type of drink, the type in which you drop one liquid into another liquid, then drink them both together ●

Lemon Drop Shooter

INGREDIENTS

Ice
Sugar to rim glass
1 ounce citrus vodka
$\frac{1}{2}$ ounce triple sec
$\frac{1}{2}$ ounce lemon juice
$\frac{1}{2}$ ounce simple syrup
Sugared lemon (optional)

1. Shake the ingredients with ice and strain into a 3–5-ounce sugar-rimmed shooter glass.

It's rumored that this way of serving shooters evolved after the "martini craze" of the late 1990s. Before that, bartenders would some-times serve rounds of shooters in cocktail/martini glasses (mostly to women). So, really, the flavored sipping martinis of today are just the gulping shooters of yesterday.

Melon Ball

INGREDIENTS

Ice
1 ounce vodka
½ ounce melon liqueur
1 ounce orange juice

1. Shake ingredients with ice.

2. Strain into a 3–5-ounce shooter glass.

Some people like to replace the orange juice with pineapple juice.

SoCo Lime

INGREDIENTS

Ice
1½ ounces Southern Comfort
½ ounce Rose's lime cordial

1. Shake ingredients with ice.

2. Strain into a 3–5-ounce shooter glass.

Members of the millennium J-Lo genera-
tion may think they were hip and trendy by
combining Southern Comfort and lime juice
and naming the result "SoCo and Lime," but
if Janis Joplin were alive today she'd have a
few things to say about that. She was drinking Southern Comfort and Lime in the 1960s
and made it well known that it was her drink
of choice.

Kamikaze

INGREDIENTS

Ice
1 ounce vodka
1/2 ounce triple sec
1/2 ounce Rose's lime cordial

1. Shake ingredients with ice.

2. Strain into a 3–5-ounce shooter glass.

Kamikaze is a Japanese word. *Kami* means "God/divine," and *kaze* means "wind." In the late 1200s, Mongolia tried to invade Japan, but a typhoon killed the Mongolian invaders. The Japanese interpreted the typhoon as a gift from God. The Kamikaze shooter, however, did not get its name from the typhoon.

Blue Kamikaze

INGREDIENTS

Ice
1 ounce vodka
½ ounce blue Curaçao
½ ounce Rose's lime cordial

1. Shake ingredients with ice.

2. Strain into a 3–5-ounce shooter glass.

Basically a Kamikaze is just a vodka gimlet with triple sec. And if you add cranberry juice, then you can call it a "cosmopolitan." These modern Kamikaze versions bump up the flavor value in a big way.

Raspberry Kamikaze

INGREDIENTS

Ice
1 ounce raspberry vodka
$\frac{1}{2}$ ounce Chambord
$\frac{1}{2}$ ounce Rose's lime cordial

1. Shake ingredients with ice.

2. Strain into a 3–5-ounce shooter glass.

Cherry Kamikaze

INGREDIENTS

Ice
1 ounce cherry vodka
$1/2$ ounce triple sec
$1/2$ ounce Rose's lime cordial
Cherry garnish

1. Shake ingredients with ice.

2. Strain into a 3-5-ounce shooter glass. Add garnish.

These flavored Kamikazes can jumpstart a world of possibilities because so many flavors go well with lime. Secondly, there are many flavored vodkas to choose from. You can also make Rainbow Kamikazes by secretly dropping one drop of food coloring into glasses. As you strain the Kamikazes into the glasses, your friends will be amazed how each drink comes out a different color.

Purple Hooter

INGREDIENTS

Ice
1 ounce vodka
$\frac{1}{2}$ ounce raspberry liqueur
$\frac{1}{2}$ ounce lemon juice
$\frac{1}{2}$ ounce simple syrup

1. Shake ingredients with ice.

2. Strain into a 3–5-ounce shooter glass.

For the Purple Hooter you could use half citrus vodka and half raspberry vodka.

Raspberry Burst

INGREDIENTS

1 ounce raspberry flavored vodka
$^3/_4$ ounce peach schnapps
$^1/_4$ ounce cranberry juice

1. Shake the vodka and schnapps with ice.

2. Strain into a shooter glass.

Hollywood

INGREDIENTS

Ice
1 ounce vodka
$\frac{1}{2}$ ounce raspberry liqueur
1 ounce pineapple juice

1. Shake ingredients with ice.

2. Strain into a 3–5-ounce shooter glass.

For the Hollywood, try also pineapple and raspberry vodka.

Purple Haze

INGREDIENTS

$1/2$ ounce Sambuca
$1/2$ ounce Chambord

1. Pour the Sambuca into a shot glass.

2. Add the Chambord very slowly. Do not mix.

There are a lot of raspberry liqueurs on the market, but Chambord Liqueur Royale de France is the ultimate raspberry liqueur. No other raspberry liqueur can compare with its taste. It has been made in the Loire River valley of France since the late 1600s with black raspberries, Madagascar vanilla, Moroccan citrus peel, honey, cognac, and, of course, some secret ingredients. It was a favorite drink for royal gatherings. The bottle is not like any other liqueur bottle in the world, with its round shape adorned with a gold band, then topped with a gold crown cap.

Nuts and Berries

INGREDIENTS

Ice
1 ounce raspberry liqueur
1 ounce Frangelico
1 ounce half-and-half

1. Shake ingredients with ice.

2. Strain into a 3–5-ounce shooter glass.

For the Nuts and Berries, know that you can substitute whole, 2 percent, 1 percent, skim, or soy milk.

Bling Bling

INGREDIENTS

$1/2$ ounce butterscotch schnapps
$1/2$ ounce raspberry flavored vodka

1. Shake the vodka and schnapps with ice.

2. Strain into a shooter glass.

If these shooters sound like they'd make a nice, tall, cool cocktail, you're right! All you have to do is fill a tall glass with ice, add the alcohol, fill with the mixer, and stir. It works the other way, too. Have a favorite cocktail? Well, make a shooter out of it by reducing the mixer amount.

Woo Woo

INGREDIENTS

Ice
1 ounce vodka
1 ounce peach schnapps
1 ounce cranberry juice

1. Shake ingredients with ice.

2. Strain into a 3–5-ounce shooter glass.

3. You're supposed to drink this shooter, then yell, "Woo woo!"

White cranberries are harvested about three weeks before they turn red. White cranberry juice hit the market after the grape industry came out with white grape juice. You can easily make a white Woo Woo by substituting regular cranberry juice with white cranberry juice. You can also find flavored white cranberry juice in peach and strawberry flavors.

Red Snapper

INGREDIENTS

Ice
1 ounce Crown Royal
1 ounce Amaretto
1 ounce cranberry juice

1. Shake ingredients with ice.

2. Strain into a 3–5-ounce shooter glass.

The Scarlett O'Hara (Southern Comfort and cranberry juice with a lime) was the first popular cranberry cocktail. It was created for the 1939 film *Gone with the Wind*.

Red Headed German

INGREDIENTS

Ice
1 ounce Jägermeister
1 ounce peach schnapps
1 ounce cranberry juice

1. Shake ingredients with ice.

2. Strain into a 3–5-ounce shooter glass.

Today you can find cranberry blends at your local grocery store in the following flavors: apple, cherry, grape, mango, raspberry, strawberry, and tangerine, which, by the way, opens a whole world of possibilities in substituting regular cranberry juice for any of the shooter recipes included here.

Vampire

INGREDIENTS

1 ounce Chambord
1 ounce vodka
1 ounce cranberry juice

1. Shake the Chambord, vodka, and juice with ice.

2. Strain into a shooter glass.

Surfer on Acid

INGREDIENTS

Ice
1 ounce Jägermeister
$\frac{1}{2}$ ounce coconut rum
1 ounce pineapple juice

1. Shake ingredients with ice.

2. Strain into a 3–5-ounce shooter glass.

If not for Sidney E. Frank, the word *Jägermeister* would probably not be part of your vocabulary. He was the genius who imported and marketed this German herbal liqueur in the 1970s. And what better way to sell lots of product than to create a novelty machine to go with it! That's when the Jägermeister tap machine was born. This machine chills the Jäger to 28°F. Sidney knew that the key to marketing is to target pop culture. So he promoted Jäger by becoming the tour sponsor for Mötley Crüe, Metallica, and a list of underground bands. He then started the annual Jägermeister Music Tour.

Monkey's Lunch

INGREDIENTS

Ice
1 ounce banana liqueur
1 ounce coffee liqueur
1 ounce half-and-half

1. Shake ingredients with ice.

2. Strain into a 3–5-ounce shooter glass.

Mind Eraser

INGREDIENTS

Ice
1 ounce coffee liqueur
1/2 ounce vodka
4 ounces soda water

1. Fill a highball glass with ice.

2. Pour the ingredients in order into the glass.

3. Drink fast with a straw.

The Mind Eraser has been around since the 1980s. Its novelty lies in the fact that you drink it really fast through a straw. Some people put two straws together. You can give it a modern update by using flavored vodkas such as vanilla, chocolate, orange, or raspberry. You could also substitute the coffee liqueur for espresso liqueur to give it an extra kick.

Undertow

INGREDIENTS

$1/2$ ounce blue Curaçao
$1/2$ ounce raspberry schnapps

1. Pour blue Curaçao into shot glass.

2. Without mixing, add the schnapps.

Irish Boilermaker

INGREDIENTS

$^3/_4$ ounce Irish whiskey
$^3/_4$ ounce Baileys Original Irish Cream
6 ounces Guinness Stout

1. Pour the first two ingredients into a shot glass.

2. Pour the stout into a pint glass.

3. Drop the shot into the pint glass.

Lunch Box

INGREDIENTS

$^3/_4$ ounce Southern Comfort
$^3/_4$ ounce Amaretto
3 ounces lager beer
3 ounces orange juice

1. Pour the first two ingredients into a shot glass.

2. Pour the beer and juice into a pint glass.

3. Drop the shot into the pint glass.

The Boilermaker started with two simple parts: a shot of whiskey followed by a chaser of beer. Today a Boilermaker has turned into a type of drink, the type in which you drop one liquid into another liquid, then drink them both together.

Flaming Dr Pepper

INGREDIENTS

6 ounces lager beer
1 ounce Amaretto
$\frac{1}{2}$ ounce 151 rum

1. Pour the beer into a pint glass.

2. Pour the other ingredients in order into a shot glass. Light.

3. Drop the flaming shot into the pint glass.

Tulane University students have been known to drop a shot of half citrus vodka and half blue Curaçao into a pilsner beer. The beer turns green, which matches their mascot, the Green Wave.

Jäger Bomb

INGREDIENTS

4 ounces Red Bull energy drink
$1^1/_2$ ounces Jägermeister

1. Pour the Red Bull into a highball glass.

2. Pour the Jägermeister into a shot glass.

3. Drop the shot into the pint glass.

Other Boilermakers you can try are a Sake Bomb (sake dropped into Japanese beer), Jackknife (Jack Daniel's dropped into beer), Canadian Car Bomb (Canadian whisky and maple syrup dropped into Canadian beer), and a Russian Ruffe (vodka dropped into beer).

Chocolate Shot Glasses

To make chocolate shot glasses, you will need 3-ounce paper cups, 1-ounce plastic portion cups, a double boiler (or microwave), a cookie sheet, unflavored cooking spray, baking chocolate, and baker's wax. Start with small batches at first to get the hang of it.

1. Melt the chocolate and baker's wax in a double boiler or microwave.
2. Spray the insides of the 3-ounce cups and the outsides of the 1-ounce cups with the cooking spray to prevent sticking.
3. Pour the melted chocolate $^3/_4$ of the way up the 3-ounce cup, then push the 1-ounce cup into the chocolate until the chocolate oozes to the top. This molds the inside of the shot glass.
4. Place onto the cookie sheet and freeze to set.
5. When ready, remove from the freezer and pop off the portion cups.

The 1-ounce portion cups can be found at candy, wedding, and restaurant supply stores.